Published in 2022 by OH!
An Imprint of Welbeck Non-Fiction Limited,
part of Welbeck Publishing Group.

Based in London and Sydney.
www.welbeckpublishing.com

Compilation text © Welbeck Non-Fiction Limited 2022
Design © Welbeck Non-Fiction Limited 2022

Disclaimer:
This book is intended for general informational purposes only and should not be relied upon as recommending or promoting any specific practice, diet or method of treatment. It is not intended to diagnose, advise, treat or prevent any illness or condition and is not a substitute for advice from a professional practitioner of the subject matter contained in this book. You should not use the information in this book as a substitute for medication, nutritional, diet, spiritual or other treatment that is prescribed by your practitioner. The publisher makes no representations or warranties with respect to the accuracy, completeness or currency of the contents of this work, and specifically disclaim, without limitation, any implied warranties of merchantability or fitness for a particular purpose and any injury, illness, damage, death, liability or loss incurred, directly or indirectly from the use or application of any of the contents of this book. Furthermore, the publisher is not affiliated with and does not sponsor or endorse any uses of or beliefs about in any way referred in this book.

ISBN 978-1-80069-180-3

Compiled, written and designed by: RH
Editorial: Victoria Godden
Project manager: Russell Porter
Production: Jess Brisley

A CIP catalogue record for this book is available from the British Library

Printed in China

10 9 8 7 6 5 4 3 2 1

Illustrations: Freepik.com

THE LITTLE BOOK ABOUT

CHEESE

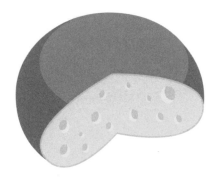

MATURED TO PERFECTION

CONTENTS

INTRODUCTION

Cheese is one of the most popular foods in the world, and has been so for centuries – millennia even. But what is it that is so enjoyable about milk that's been soured, treated, washed and heated, then (often) left to mature before we eat it – in a wide variety of different ways? You can cut up a piece of cheese and eat it by itself. You can add a cracker, some fruit or put it on bread. You can make a sandwich or drop some in salad. And that's before you've even started to heat it or cook with it. You can grate it, grill it, melt it – there are near countless ways to enjoy this simple, natural food.

And also – as any cheese-lover knows – eating cheese is not simply eating. It's convivial, social, enjoyable and comes with its own culture, vocabulary and tools.

Nearly every country in the world makes cheese, be that a form of factory-made Cheddar (one of the most popular), or hand-made artisan cheeses – and everything in between. And they all give us a simple slice of pleasure wherever we are, whoever we are with and whatever the time of day.

So, please relish in this book as you would your cheese – and savour every page.

CHAPTER
ONE

On the Origin of Cheeses

Mankind's relationship with cheese dates back thousands of years, and of course relates closely to the keeping of cattle and livestock. People who kept cows, sheep and goats realized they had a stock of not just milk, but milk products, the greatest of which was cheese...

Historical evidence dates cheese production as early as 8000BCE and the oldest known cheese was found in China, dating back to 1615BCE.

Ancient Greek philosopher Epicurus once requested "a wheel of **hard cheese**" in a letter to his patron.

HOW CHEESE IS MADE
Step 1:

Milk is heated up (or used straight from a cow/goat/sheep).

66

It is said that Zoroaster lived 30 years in the wilderness upon cheese, prepared in such a peculiar manner, that he was insensible to the advances of old age.

99

The Natural History, 77CE, Pliny the Elder.

HOW CHEESE IS MADE
Step 2:

The milk is acidified, by the addition of vinegar, citric acid or live cultures.

Cheeses can be
washed in **beer**,
cider, **wine** or
even **brandy**
to give a fuller
flavour.

HOW CHEESE IS MADE
Step 3:

A coagulant (rennet) is added, in order to form a curd.

"

The King's cheese
is half wasted in
pairings: But no
matter, 'tis made of
the people's milk.

"

The Autobiography and Other Writings,
Benjamin Franklin

HOW CHEESE IS MADE
Step 4:

The curd is cut into smaller pieces and stirred (usually heated up as well).

In Roman times, some large houses had separate cheesemaking kitchens, named *careale*.

HOW CHEESE IS MADE
Step 5:

The curd is drained, and separated from the whey.

The word **cheese** comes from the Old English, *cēse*. It is related to the Dutch word *kaas* and German *Käse*, and its origins are in the Latin *caseus*, meaning "to ferment".

HOW CHEESE IS MADE
Step 6:

A shape is formed. You can now eat the cheese (or compress it, leave it, add salt, or mature it.)

October is American Cheese Month.

In England in the 16th Century, when Henry VIII closed down monasteries, cheese consumption suffered, as they were important centres of the craft.

Edam, a cheese that originates from the Netherlands, is one of the most instantly recognizable due to its covering, or rind, of red paraffin wax.

The fact that it does not spoil (it only hardens over time), combined with its ability to travel well over long distances, made it the most popular cheese between the 14th and 18th centuries.

> **"**
>
> A corpse is meat gone bad. Well and what's cheese? Corpse of Milk.
>
> **"**

Ulysses, 1922, James Joyce

Cheese can be made
with milk from
cows, sheep, goats –
and even
donkey, moose and
camel milk.

Thomas Jefferson
first brought
mac & cheese
to America.

In the Bible,
David carried
cheese to his
troops before he
slayed Goliath.

66

Cheese has always been a food that both sophisticated and simple humans love.

99

The Art of Eating, 1954, M.F.K. Fisher

The first
cheese factory was
opened in

1815,

in
Switzerland.

More than 400 Australian cheeses were tasted by judges at the 2020 Grand Dairy Awards.

The grand champion was Berry's Creek Oak Blue.

Australian Grand Dairy Awards Champions 2020

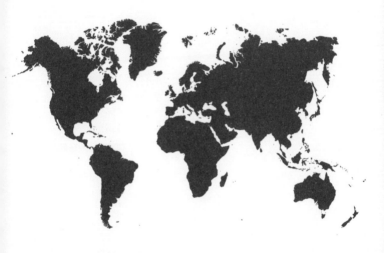

Cheese is made in
all regions of the world.

Dating back to 3000BC, a frieze
found at the Temple of the Great
Goddess of Life, Ninhursag,
in Mesopotamia, provides the
earliest pictorial evidence for
cheesemaking.
It shows cows being milked on
one side, and butter being churned
and strained on the other.

China is one of the lowest consumers of cheese per capita, alongside South Korea, South Africa, Colombia and Zimbabwe.

Turophile

is the word for a cheese lover.

In medieval times it was common to make cheese in an animal's stomach filled with milk, strapped to the back of a horse.

The natural rennet and motion would cause curds to form.

66

People who know
nothing about cheeses reel
away from Camembert,
Roquefort, and Stilton
because the plebeian
proboscis is not equipped
to differentiate between the
sordid and the sublime.

Harvey Day

Plymouth,
Wisconsin, in the
USA, is known
as the
**Cheese Capital of
the World.**

Annual cheese
production in the US
exceeded
2 billion pounds
(900m kg)
of cheese by 1990.

International Dairy Foods Association

Thanks to mass-produced rennet and the development of pure microbial cultures around 1900, cheesemaking became standardized and factory-made cheese became the norm, overtaking traditional, artisanal cheesemaking by WWII.

66

French emperor
Charlemagne was keen on
cheese. In a famous story he
is encouraged to eat the
mould by an archbishop.
He asks for "two cartloads of
such cheese" to be sent
to him each year.

99

On Food and Cooking: The Science and Lore of the Kitchen,
2007, Harold McGee

President Andrew Jackson once had a Cheddar cheese that weighed 1,400 pounds (635kg) delivered to the White House.

In 1851, dairy farmer Jesse Williams started to make cheese on an industrial scale in Rome, New York.

Edam cheese was used
as cannonballs in a
battle between
Montevido, Uruguay
and Buenos Aires
in 1841.
One even managed to kill
two soldiers.

Age is something that does not matter, unless you are a cheese.

My Last Sigh, 1983, Luis Buñuel

Three countries in Europe show the earliest evidence of cheesemaking:

Poland, **Croatia** and **Switzerland**.

CHAPTER
TWO

Grate Things About Cheese

Fascinating facts, delicious details and all manner of cheese-related information...

It usually takes approximately 10 pounds (4.5kg) of milk to make 1 pound (.5kg) of cheese.

Wisconsin
produces the
greatest amount
of cheese in the USA,
California is second.

According to research from the Academy of General Dentistry in the USA, eating cheese can prevent tooth decay because it neutralizes acid in the mouth.

Legend says that cheeses were traditionally round so cheesemakers could roll them to deliveries instead of carrying them.

The Credito Emiliano bank
in the Emilia-Romagna region
of Northern Italy accepts wheels
of parmesan cheese as collateral
from farmers looking to secure
small monetary loans.

At last count, it had more than
300,000 wheels in its vaults –
worth well over 160 million euros
back in 2017.

The winner of the 2020 World Champion Cheese Contest was **Gourmino Le Gruyère AOP** from Switzerland.

A law in Wisconsin
once required
cheese & butter
to be served with all meals
in restaurants.

It was only effective
between June 1935 and
March 1937.

The Wheeler Report, reported on wisblawg.law.wisc.edu

A 2005 study by the
British Cheese Board
found that eating cheese
shortly before going to
bed could possibly help
you sleep better.

One of Queen Victoria's wedding presents was a Cheddar cheese that weighed more than 1,000 pounds (453kg).

The most popular
cheese globally
is Cheddar, then
Mozzarella.

66

I was one of those.
I meddled with dark
powers. I summoned
demons. I ate the
entire little cheese,
including the rind.

99

The Wise Man's Fear, 2011, Patrick Rothfuss

The world's biggest
cheese is a huge Cheddar
made in Wisconsin, USA
in 1988.

It weighed
40,000 pounds
(18,000kg).

The most expensive cheese in
the world is
pule donkey cheese,
and will set you back
£450, ($600) for just one kilogram.

There's only one place that makes it – a
farm in the Zasavica Special Nature
Reserve, Serbia – and it requires over
24 litres (6½ gallons) of donkey milk to
make 1kg (2.2lbs) of cheese.

Safe to say, it's a long and, er,
unique process...

In the USA, the market for processed cheese is larger than factory-made cheese.

On Food and Cooking, 2004, Harold McGee

CHAPTER
THREE

The Wonderful World of Cheese

There are more than 2,000 different kinds of cheese in the world, with a large number of variations. In this chapter we examine just a small selection of the greatest, most pungent and popular cheeses you can eat.

Brie

Origin: **France**
Milk: **Cow**
Type: **Soft**

Brie is produced in many places around the world, but the protected Brie de Meaux and Brie de Melun are still hugely popular, and both made with unpasteurized cheese and matured for longer than most of their impersonators.

Berry's Creek
Oak Blue

Origin: **Australia**
Milk: **Cow**
Type: **Blue**

This Gorgonzola-style cheese is made
by the artisans at Berry's Creek in
Australia using non-animal rennet.
It is a heavily veined blue cheese and is
highly regarded for good reason, with
subtle flavour and great taste.

Burrata

Origin: **Italy**
Milk: **Cow**
Type: **Soft**

Best described as a skin of Mozzarella filled with cream and more Mozzarella, Burrata is a creamy, delicious treat of a cheese. The fresher the better for this cheese, which can be eaten alone or with salads, and is popular on pizza in some regions.

Caerphilly

Origin: **Wales**
Milk: **Cow**
Type: **Hard**

Originally only made in Wales, but now produced in England (with milk from Welsh cows), Caerphilly is a subtly flavoured, crumbly cheese that goes especially well with oat crackers and fruit. Very distinctive white colour, taste and texture.

Camembert

Origin: **France**
Milk: **Cow**
Type: **Soft**

This cheese, produced in Normandy in northern France is one of the world's great cheeses and is very versatile.
It can be eaten young, with a chalky, hard texture; mature versions are more creamy and tend to be stronger in flavour. Edible rind, bakes well.

Canastra

Origin: **Brazil**
Milk: **Cow**
Type: **Semi-hard**

The Brazilian state of Minas Gerais is the home of this cheese, specifically the area of Serra da Canastra. Quite hard in texture, the flavour is a little spicy and salty. Ideal for accompanying pasta but fine to be enjoyed alone or as part of a platter.

Cascaval afumat

Origin: **Romania**
Milk: **Cow**
Type: **Semi-soft**

With a slightly bitter taste and rubbery texture, this smoked cheese pairs well with meats when eaten alone, or can be fried, grilled or barbecued to good effect.

Cashel Blue

Origin: **Ireland**
Milk: **Cow**
Type: **Blue**

A tangy, creamy blue cheese that ages well to maturity, Cashel Blue is produced in Tipperary Eire. It is great for cooking as well as enjoying alone. A relatively modern cheese, it was created in the late twentieth century by Louis and Jane Grubb; it is still made by hand in the same location.

Cheddar

Origin: **Great Britain**
Milk: **Cow**
Type: **Hard**

So many types of Cheddar exist it's impossible to list them all. From factory-produced, bland cheeses to hand-made, delicious treats that rank among the best in the world, Cheddar has many different guises. The original is still matured in caves in Cheddar Gorge in Southwest England.

Colby

Origin: **USA**
Milk: **Cow**
Type: **Semi-hard**

A very popular cheese in the USA,
Colby has a distinctive flavour and
colour, which comes from annatto
seasoning. A highly versatile cheese,
Colby is commonly used to adorn
anything from burgers to quesadillas.

Comté

Origin: **France**
Milk: **Cow**
Type: **Hard**

A versatile, salty hard cheese, Comté is enjoyed as a young cheese when fresh, and in a much stronger, dryer version when aged. Great with nuts and fruit and it is an excellent cooking cheese.

Cotija

Origin: **Mexico**
Milk: **Cow**
Type: **Semi-hard**

Produced in Michoacàn, this semi-hard and very crumbly cheese is very salty in flavour and is only produced seasonally in limited quantities. Often used for cooking – commonly grated or crumbled onto hot food – it can also be eaten alone.

Edam

Origin: **The Netherlands**
Milk: **Cow**
Type: **Semi-hard**

With its distinctive red waxed coating, Edam is as versatile as it is extremely mild. Superb for cooking, with a slight nutty flavour, it is delicious with fruit and is a very mild cheese.

Emmental

Origin: **Switzerland**
Milk: **Cow**
Type: **Hard**

A delightfully mild, nutty cheese, Emmental is the cook's choice for many countries in western Europe but is also very tasty when served alone. Great for fondue and other cooking, and it is often overlooked on a cheese platter, where it is a solid performer.

Epoisses

Origin: **France**
Milk: **Cow**
Type: **Soft**

The distinct colour, smell and taste of Epoisses come from its being washed in local brandy as part of the manufacturing process. So soft it can be eaten with a spoon, or as an 'instant fondue' with a quick blast in the oven.

Feta

Origin: **Greece**
Milk: **Sheep**
Type: **Soft**

A salty, crumbly soft cheese, Feta is hugely popular all over the world and goes extremely well with a large number of foodstuffs. It is often mixed into salads, where its texture and flavour combine perfectly with other ingredients.

Gorgonzola

Origin: **Italy**
Milk: **Cow**
Type: **Blue/soft**

A surprisingly strong, creamy, blue cheese, Gorgonzola goes well with a wide variety of foodstuffs and cooking techniques.

Gouda

Origin: **The Netherlands**
Milk: **Cow**
Type: **Hard**

One of the oldest cheeses in the world, Gouda is also one of the most popular. Most is factory made, but handmade versions still exist. This distinctive yellow cheese is usually sold aged for up to 36 months.

Gruyère

Origin: **Switzerland**
Milk: **Cow**
Type: **Hard**

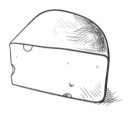

A classic cheese with origins in the 12th century, Gruyère is a kitchen essential and is excellent when melted into a fondue, or eaten solo.

Halloumi

Origin: **Cyprus**
Milk: **Sheep/goat**
Type: **Hard**

A very distinctive, salty cheese that
is usually cooked or heated before
serving and works well on a barbecue.
It is responsible for one of the most
dangerously delicious foodstuffs known
to mankind: halloumi fries.

Jarlsberg

Origin: **Norway**
Milk: **Cow**
Type: **Semi-hard**

Mild and buttery, this Norwegian cheese is a great all-rounder, comfortable melted on a burger and stands up well on a cheese board as well as a snack.

Limburger

Origin: **Germany**
Milk: **Cow**
Type: **Semi-soft**

Most of the cheese that bears the
Limburger name is now produced in
Germany despite origins of the name in
Belgium and The Netherlands too. The
cheese ages well, from being firm and
crumbly when fresh to a more creamy,
smoother cheese when matured.

Manchego

Origin: **Spain**
Milk: **Sheep**
Type: **Hard**

Probably the most famous Spanish cheese, Manchego comes from the La Mancha region and its Manchega sheep. Traditionally served with quince jelly and aged for a minimum of 60 days, the rind of this slightly bitter but utterly delicious, subtle cheese is not edible.

Mascarpone

Origin: **Italy**
Milk: **Cow**
Type: **Cream cheese**

A cream cheese that's made from, well, cream, Mascarpone is very rich and is often used as an ingredient for other dishes, including tiramisu, cheesecake or risotto.

Monterey Jack

Origin: **USA**
Milk: **Cow**
Type: **Semi-hard**

A very tasty, original American cheese that was first made in California. Mild and sweet, it makes a very viable alternative to Cheddar. It is believed to have been made originally by monks.

Morbier

Origin: **France**
Milk: **Cow**
Type: **Semi-hard/
  Blue**

Fabricated in small wheels, this
unique cheese has a layer of ash
running through the centre, which
counterbalances the smooth flavour
and texture of it. A few holes contribute
further, making this a real treat.

Mori No

Origin: **Japan**
Milk: **Cow**
Type: **Hard**

Swiss cows were imported to Japan and they graze on mountain pastures in their new home in Matsumoto.
A hand-made hard cheese with occasional eyes, Mori No is highly regarded and critically acclaimed.

Mozzarella

Origin: **Italy**
Milk: **Buffalo**
Type: **Semi-soft**

Traditionally served very fresh (the day after it is made), Mozzarella has become the go-to pizza cheese but is an ideal accompaniment to many other foods. It can also be made with cow, goat or sheep milk. Originated in Italy, possibly as far back as 1200CE.

Paneer

Origin: **India**
Milk: **Buffalo/cow**
Type: **Semi-hard**

Usually used as an addition to other dishes, this interesting cheese mixes beautifully with spicy dishes and works well on a barbecue.

Parmesan

Origin: **Italy**
Milk: **Cow**
Type: **Hard**

A classic accompaniment to many dishes, this salty Italian cheese is delicious and is popular all over the world but made only in Italy, where it enjoys protected status.

Pecorino Romano

Origin: **Italy**
Milk: **sheep**
Type: **Hard**

Almost exclusively used as an accompaniment to pasta dishes, Pecorino is produced in various regions of Italy. Nutty and less salty than Parmesan, it can be eaten solo.

Processed cheese

Origin: **USA**
Milk: **Cow**
Type: **Soft**

Processed cheese is so popular all around the world that it gets a slot in this list. Technically 'cheese food' rather than actual cheese, it tends to be individually wrapped ready to place in a sandwich or dish.

Provolone

Origin: **Italy**
Milk: **Cow**
Type: **Hard**

Commonly sold in small, roundish
balls, this hard, sharp cheese comes
in many varieties, including "picante",
which is aged and "dolce", which is not.

Queijo Serra da Estrela

Origin: **Portugal**
Milk: **Sheep**
Type: **Soft**

A very soft cheese with a creamy interior and soft skin, the cheese is an international classic from Portugal. It is made from raw ewe's milk.

Reblochon

Origin: **France**
Milk: **Cow**
Type: **Soft**

Made in the Savoie Alpine region of France, this cheese is famously used in the winter dish tartiflette, where a whole cheese is baked into a mixture of potatoes, bacon and cream. Very earthy flavour with edible rind, it is delicious alone as well.

Roquefort

Origin: **France**
Milk: **Sheep**
Type: **Blue/soft**

Strong, creamy and salty, with blue
veins of natural bacteria, Roquefort
is one of the most distinct cheeses.
Often used for cooking, it is a very fine
standalone cheese too.

Saint-Nectaire

Origin: **France**
Milk: **Cow**
Type: **Semi-hard**

A pressed farm cheese made in the Augergne region of France, Saint-Nectaire is matured for a minimum of six weeks. The result is a delightful mixture of sweet and bitter flavours and a super-smooth texture. Delicious with a fresh baguette.

San Michali

Origin: **Greece (Syros)**
Milk: **Cow**
Type: **Hard**

A hard cheese with a buttery flavour, San Michali is solely produced on the island of Syros with milk from local cows. A little spicy in taste, it can be used for cooking or enjoyed alone or with fruit.

Stilton

Origin: **Great Britain**
Milk: **Cow**
Type: **Blue**

Produced only in three regions of the UK: Derbyshire, Leicestershire and Nottinghamshire, Stilton is a very versatile cheese with many different varieties and flavours. Excellent for cooking as well as with crackers or even ginger biscuits.

Stinking Bishop

Origin: **Great Britain**
Milk: **Cow**
Type: **Soft**

A relatively new cheese, launched in 1994 by Charles Martell & Son Ltd, this full fat soft cheese is washed in perry to give its heavy aroma. Smooth, sticky and impressively odorous, it comes in a number of different sizes, each one delicious.

Västerbotten

Origin: **Sweden**
Milk: **Cow**
Type: **Hard**

A Cheddar-like cheese that is manufactured in Sweden, Västerbotten is very tasty, salty but sweet, with a hard texture. Great for eating alone or for cooking, this is a very versatile cheese from an uncommon source.

Vieux Boulogne

Origin: **France**
Milk: **Cow**
Type: **Soft**

With a bright orange rind that's washed in beer, this is a tasty but very odorous cheese indeed. Has been referred to as "the world's smelliest cheese" and if you are lucky enough to try some of this artisan cheese you'll know why.

CHAPTER
FOUR

Cheese the Day!

Words of wisdom, amusing quotations and inspirational sayings, all related to cheese.

66

How can you govern a country that has 246 varieties of cheese?

99

Charles de Gaulle, former President of France

International
Cheese-lover's Day
is on

January

20

66

A dessert without cheese is a beauty with only one eye.

99

Jean Anthelme Brillat-Savarin (1755–1826),
French lawyer and politician

Collecting
cheese labels
is called
tyrosemiophilia.

66

Hast thou not poured me out as milk, and curdled me like cheese?

99

Job 10:10, King James Bible

66

You can't make everyone happy; you're not cheese.

99

Anonymous

66
You Banbury Cheese!
99

Bardolph to Abraham Slender, *The Merry Wives of Windsor*,
William Shakespeare

66

A country without a fit drink for cheese has no cheese fit for drink.

99

Ancient Greek proverb

"
... blessed are the cheesemakers.
"

Monty Python's Life of Brian

66

What a friend
we have in cheeses.

99

David Lange, former Prime Minister of New Zealand

The clever cat eats cheese and breathes down rat holes with baited breath.

W.C. Fields

"
A slice of cheese is never just a thing to eat.
"

The French Cheese Book, 1989, Patrick Rance

"

When I ask how old your toddler is, I don't need to hear '27 months.' 'He's two' will do just fine. He's not a cheese.

"

George Carlin

66

Beauty is a
valuable asset,
but it is not the
whole cheese.

99

Ginger Rogers

66

A cheese may disappoint.
It may be dull, it may
be naïve, it may be over
sophisticated. Yet it
remains cheese, milk's
leap towards immortality.

99

Any Number Can Play, 1957, Clifton Fadiman

"

The early bird gets
the worm... but
the second mouse
gets the cheese.

"

Unknown

66

If you are like me – clever, fond of **goat cheese**, and devilishly handsome – then you have undoubtedly read many books.

99

Alcatraz Versus the Evil Librarians, 2007,
Brandon Sanderson

I never
met a problem
that cheese
couldn't solve.

CHAPTER
FIVE

In Queso Emergency

Eating cheese is so much more than just having a tasty bite. You can enjoy cheese in so many ways, in so many places and with so many people... or all alone.

66

It's OK if cheese is one of your best friends.

99

Cheese tastes best
when served at
**room
temperature,**
not straight from
the fridge.

Casu Martzu

cheese from Sardinia
is made with larvae
from the cheese fly and
is traditionally eaten
with the maggots
still alive.

Kurt

cheese comes in small,
white balls and
is traditional fare in
Central Asia, where it
has been eaten since the
Middle Ages.

It can be made with
horse, camel, sheep, goat
or cow's milk.

Cooper's Hill Cheese rolling, where a cheese is thrown down a steep hill and raced after, still takes place today in England, centuries after the first race.

Taking a
deep sniff of the
cheese before
you eat it enhances
the taste.

Step into any French bistro
and you'll likely find

Croque Monsieur

on the menu.

The French equivalent of grilled
cheese, its essential ingredients
are bread, cheese and ham,
although some restaurants add
creamy bechamel sauce for added
richness (and calories!).

If it has an egg
on it, a
Croque Monsiuer
becomes a
Croque Madame.

"Pasta alla ruota", or cheese wheel pasta, is made by mixing freshly cooked pasta in a hollowed wheel of parmesan, usually right in front of you.

Perfect for those who like a touch of drama with their spaghetti.

Cheese is a good
source of
calcium and **protein**,
vitamin A,
vitamin B12 and
riboflavin.

A single wheel
of parmesan cheese
takes at least one
year to age.

In Canada, the dish

poutine

is very popular.

It consists of French fries topped with melted cheese curd and gravy, although there are countless variations.

Flor de Guía,

a soft cheese made
in the Canary Islands,
must only be made
by women, or else it is
not considered the
genuine article.

66

For the very best,
drink milk from the
goat, ricotta from
the sheep and cheese
from the cow.

99

Sicilian proverb

"

Give me a good sharp knife and a good sharp cheese and I'm a happy man.

"

George R. R. Martin, **author of** *Game of Thrones*

66

I'm addicted to cheese and sugar... When they ask me if I want dinner, I'm like, 'No, I want Brie and crackers.

99

Courtney Love, Style.com, 2014

"

Claret dear, not Coca-Cola, When we're having Gorgonzola

"

What a friend we have in cheeses!,
William Rossa Cole

66

[Cheese] is synonymous
with comfort, especially
when melted, and it plays
a part in the conviviality
with raclettes or more
refined meals.

99

Les Marchés magazine, as reported in
The Guardian, March 15, 2021

Welsh rarebit originated in England in the 18th century. Essentially, it consists of some cheese on a piece of toasted bread.

66

What happens
to the hole when the
cheese is gone?

99

Bertolt Brecht

Cheese & Wine:

Soft cheese goes best with
crisp white wine.

Semi-hard and **medium** cheeses
go best with **medium-bodied**
wine.

Hard and **mature** cheeses taste
best with **full-bodied white** wine.

Blue cheese goes well with
sweet wine.

Smelly cheeses go well with
light-bodied wine.

Many cheeses made
from unpasteurized milk
are banned in the USA
(and other countries),
including
Brie de Meaux,
Roquefort and **Morbier**.

"

I'm just a regular 16-year-old kid. I make good grilled cheese and I like girls.

"

Justin Bieber

"

Pasta with melted
cheese is the one
thing I could eat over
and over again.

"

Yotam Ottolenghi

If you think smelly cheese and stinky feet smell similar it's no coincidence,
as they both contain the same bacteria:

brevibacterium linens.

66

When baiting a
mousetrap
with cheese, always
leave room for the
mouse.

99

"The Infernal Parliament", 1924, Saki (H. H. Munro)

CHAPTER
SIX

Gouda Idea!

Some essential tips and tricks for cooking, serving and, more importantly, *eating* that special cheese in your life...

Although cheese should ideally be served at room temperature, store it in the vegetable crisper section of the refrigerator to make it last longer.

This is where the temperature is nice and constant, and usually a little warmer than the rest of the fridge – around 5–8°C (41–46°F).

Generally, the harder the cheese, the longer it can last. You can prolong their lifespan by wrapping them in special waxed cheese paper – the kind the cheesemonger uses – which wicks excess moisture away while also allowing it to "breathe".

Never leave cheese
uncovered in the fridge,
as you will find it soon
starts to take on the
flavour of any other foods
you've got in there.

You can save the rind of parmesan and add it to flavour stews, soups, sauces and bean dishes.

Whole rinds can be kept in the freezer until you need them, and even be made into parmesan stock – perfect for risottos.

Cheeseboard Etiquette
Rule #1

No matter how many cheeses you serve, always provide a separate knife for each one, so there's no cross-contamination of flavours.

We also recommend arranging cheeses along the board from mild to strong, so your guests have some idea of what they're slicing into.

Labelling each one can be a good idea, too.

Cheeseboard Etiquette
Rule #2

Maintain the wedge!

There is no greater cheese faux pas than to "nose" a wedge of cheese – i.e. to take the pointy end right off. Instead, let the shape of the cheese determine how you cut it.

So, if it's a whole wheel, slice it like a cake. If it's a wedge, cut it so that what's left is just a slightly smaller wedge. Rectangular blocks like feta can be cut lengthways.

Cheeseboard Etiquette
Rule #3

No mining!

It is considered very poor form to "mine" a soft cheese like brie or camembert – meaning you eat just the soft, gooey centre and leave the rind (which is perfectly edible!) for everyone else. Instead, take a whole slice and then eat whichever parts you like – just do it on your own plate!

Cheeseboard Etiquette
Rule #4

Crackers and fruit are the classic cheeseboard staples, but don't be afraid to experiment with other accompaniments.

Try dried fruits like apricots, prunes and figs, a selection of charcuterie, marinated olives, pesto and/or honey alongside your usual jams and jellies.

Cheeseboard Etiquette
Rule #5

If you're pre-cutting cheese,
make sure you don't cube it. The more
surface area there is, the more flavour
can make it to your tongue, so slices are
always preferable.

Some Great Cheese and Food Pairings

Ricotta + Honey
Brie + Pistachios
Fontana + Mushrooms
Monteray Jack + Hazelnuts
Blue + Bacon
Gorgonzola + Ginger
Cheddar + Beetroot
Gouda + Peppers
Parmesan + Balsamic Vinegar
Asiago + Fennel

Perfect Cheese Fondue
Rule #1

Rather than melting just one, choose a selection of hard mountain cheeses that have been adequately aged – vacherin fribourgeois, raclette, gruyere, comte, fontina and emmenthaler are all good examples.

Perfect Cheese Fondue
Rule #2

If you can, let your bread sit
for a day before dipping – it'll be
easier to digest with the melted
cheese that way.

Perfect Cheese Fondue
Rule #3

Melt; don't boil the cheese.

It helps to add a
little alcohol to the mix, as this lowers
its boiling point.

Perfect Cheese Fondue
Rule #4

Cheese should be cooked slowly so that it doesn't become rubbery.

If it starts to separate, turn down the heat and stir like your life depends on it. Which, let's be honest, it probably does.

Perfect Cheese Fondue
Rule #5

If your fondue mix is too thick,
simply add a splash of wine or water.

If it's too thin, add some
corn starch.

Perfect Cheese Fondue
Rule #6

Use leftover fondue
for topping potatoes, eggs or
vegetable dishes.

If you need to grate
soft cheese, pop it in the
freezer for 20 minutes
beforehand to firm it
up a little.

Grilled Cheese Sandwiches:
The Top Melters

1. Alpine cheese
2. Fontina
3. Provolone/Mozzarella
4. Cheddar
5. Raclette
6. Blue Cheese
7. Butterkäse

Instead of spreading butter on the outside of your grilled cheese sandwich, use mayonnaise.

It has a higher smoke point, so there's less chance of burning.

The Non-Melters

Some cheeses won't melt no matter how much heat you put them under, which makes them perfect for summer salads.

Some of the most popular include feta, halloumi, goat cheese, paneer, cottage cheese, mascarpone and ricotta.

GLOSSARY

Cheese Words

Essential words you will
need to know (and use) in
your quest to become a true
cheese master.

Affinage

The process of ripening or ageing a cheese, to improve the taste. Affinage is performed by an affineur.

Alpine style

A term to describe the hard, European-style cheeses typically found in mountain regions.

Ammoniated

A cheese that has a strong smell of ammonia. It can be eliminated by airing the cheese for a period of time.

Annatto

A vegetable dye that is used to introduce colour to some cheeses (Cheddar for example).

Artisanal

Usually a cheese made in small batches by a small producer. Not a factory-produced or processed cheese.

Barnyardy

A descriptive term for a cheese with aromas and flavours reminiscent of a barnyard, straw and earth pervading.

Bloomy

Soft, creamy cheeses tend to have bloomy rinds, for example Camembert. The 'bloom' is a fungus.

Bluing

The process of growing mould in cheeses, usually resulting in a stronger, sharper, more acidic taste.

Caseiculture

Basically, a flamboyant way of saying cheesemaking, or the art of making cheese.

Cheddaring

The way hard cheeses (including, but not exclusively) like cheddar are made.

Creamline

The section of a (usually) soft cheese that is found between the rind and the paste. It is commonly very creamy, hence the name.

Curds

The 'curdled' milk solids that are formed in the cheesemaking process.

Daisy

A round wheel of Cheddar, traditionally weighing 22 pounds (approx. 10kg). Will usually be cut up to distribute.

Double crème

Describes the amount of cream added to a cheese during the manufacturing process. See also triple crème.

Eyes

The "holes" in a cheese, created by bubbles in the paste.

Fermier/Ferme

Used to describe cheeses that are
produced in farms rather than
enormous factories.

Geotrichum candidum

A mould powder often added to
surface-ripened cheese to aid the
ripening process.

Marbled

A cheese in which you can see the
contrast between the various curds,
usually by the introduction of an
agent during production.

Paste

The inside of the cheese, i.e. what's under the rind (if there is one).

Pasteurized

Pasteurized milk has been heated up in order to kill potentially harmful bacteria. Some countries ban cheese made with this "raw" milk.

Raw

The opposite of pasteurized milk, where no bacteria-killing heat process has been applied before the cheese is made.

Rind

The outside bit of the cheese.
Sometimes edible, sometimes not.
Some cheeses don't have any.

Ripe

A ripe cheese is one that is just
perfect and ready to eat. Young
cheeses can be left to ripen and
develop flavour.

Sharp

A taste term for the flavour of a
cheese that is acidic.

Rennet

An enzyme that is added to milk when a cheese is made. Can be derived from animal or vegetable sources.

Surface-ripened

Bloomy rind cheeses are examples of surface-ripened, as the ripening takes place externally to start with.

Terroir

Simply put, this is the taste of a place, relating the flavour of a cheese to its original geographical location.

Tomme

A small, round cheese, usually originating from France.

Triple crème

This refers to the amount of cream added to the cheese during the manufacturing process, in this case resulting in a cheese that contains 75% fat. See also double crème.

Truckle

A wheel (see page 191) of cheese that is taller than it is wide.

Ubrico

A style of cheesemaking from Italy that involves soaking the cheese in wine for a period of time.

Washed rind

Cheeses that are, well, washed in a liquid on the outside to add flavour and (usually) smell. They tend to be the most odorous cheeses.

Wedge

A slice of cheese taken from a larger, usually round, piece.

Wheel

A big (or small) round cheese, as it is made in the factory/atelier. Usually cut up into slices for easier distribution (and eating).

Whey

The liquid that is separated from the solids (curds) during the cheesemaking process.

Wine

Alcohol that is most commonly served with cheeses. There are even more varieties of wine than there are cheese.

KEEP
CALM
AND
EAT
CHEESE